ONCE IN A BLUE MOON

Nature's Rarest Events and Best-Kept Secrets

For Hannah and Leo, with love – E.H.

To my daughter, Lily, who brings light and
wonder to my life each and every day – V.S.

Once in a Blue Moon © 2025 Quarto Publishing plc. Text © 2025 Emily Hawkins
Illustrations © 2025 Vlad Stankovic.

First Published in 2025 by Wide Eyed Editions,
an imprint of The Quarto Group.
1 Triptych Place, London, SE1 9SH, United Kingdom.
T (0)20 7700 6700 F (0)20 7700 8066 **www.Quarto.com**

The right of Emily Hawkins to be identified as the author and Vlad Stankovic to be identified as the illustrator of this work has been asserted by them in accordance with the Copyright, Designs and Patents Act, 1988 (United Kingdom).

All rights reserved.

No part of this publication may be reproduced, stored in a retrieval system, or transmitted, in any form, or by any means, electrical, mechanical, photocopying, recording or otherwise without the prior written permission of the publisher or a licence permitting restricted copying.

A catalogue record for this book is available from the British Library.

ISBN 978-0-71129-423-3

The illustrations were created digitally.
Set in Nazare and Bilo

Designers: Robyn Makings and Myrto Dimitrakoulia
Editors: Hannah Dove and Katie Taylor
Production Controller: Robin Boothroyd
Commissioning Editor: Hannah Dove
Art Director: Karissa Santos
Publisher: Debbie Foy

Manufactured in Guangdong, China TT052025

9 8 7 6 5 4 3 2 1

Emily Hawkins   Vlad Stankovic

ONCE IN A BLUE MOON

Nature's Rarest Events and
Best-Kept Secrets

WIDE EYED EDITIONS

Contents

World of Wonders — 6

Amazing Space — 8
Blue Moons & Supermoons — 10
Solar Eclipse — 12
Halley's Comet — 14
Tunguska Fireball — 16
Supernova — 18

Weird Weather — 20
Nature's Light Show — 22
Sun Dogs & Moonbows — 24
St Elmo's Fire — 26
Ball Lightning — 28
Curious Clouds — 30
Strange Snow — 32

Peculiar Plants — 34
Rare Blooming Flowers — 36
Green Giants — 38
Bleeding Trees — 40
Carnivorous Plants — 42
Extraordinary Flowers — 44
Glowing Fungi — 46

Unusual Animals — 48
Raining Fish & Frogs — 50
Uncommon Creatures — 52
Living Lights — 54
Exploding Toads — 56
Curious Colours — 58
Amazing Migrations — 60
Massive Murmurations — 62

Unique Wild Places — 64
Remarkable Rivers — 66
Strange Lakes — 68
Ocean Oddities — 70
Amazing Caves — 72
Rare Rocks — 74
Weird Volcanoes — 76

Glossary — 78
Index — 80

World of Wonders

Nature is full of surprises. Some natural events are so unusual that few people have ever witnessed them. Others are so spectacular that they inspired our ancestors to tell stories of gods and monsters. This book delves into these uncommon happenings, revealing nature's rarest events and best-kept secrets.

Within these pages you'll explore many natural wonders, and you'll discover some of the bizarre happenings that have baffled scientists: the mystery of ball lightning, the curious case of the exploding toads, and even the peculiar puzzle of creatures that seem to rain from the sky.

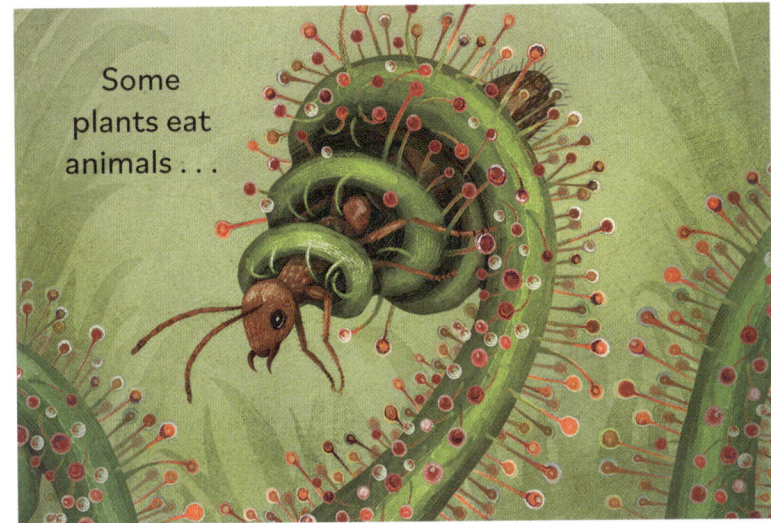

Some flowers open to reveal their beauty for only one night per year.

Some trees appear to bleed when cut.

Some plants eat animals . . .

Some animals light up like glow sticks!

In Peru, there is a river so hot that it bubbles and boils as it cascades through the forest. A volcano in Indonesia spits blue flames. Beautiful and beguiling, these rare and diverse marvels of nature have fascinated people for millennia. Prepare to explore a world of wonders.

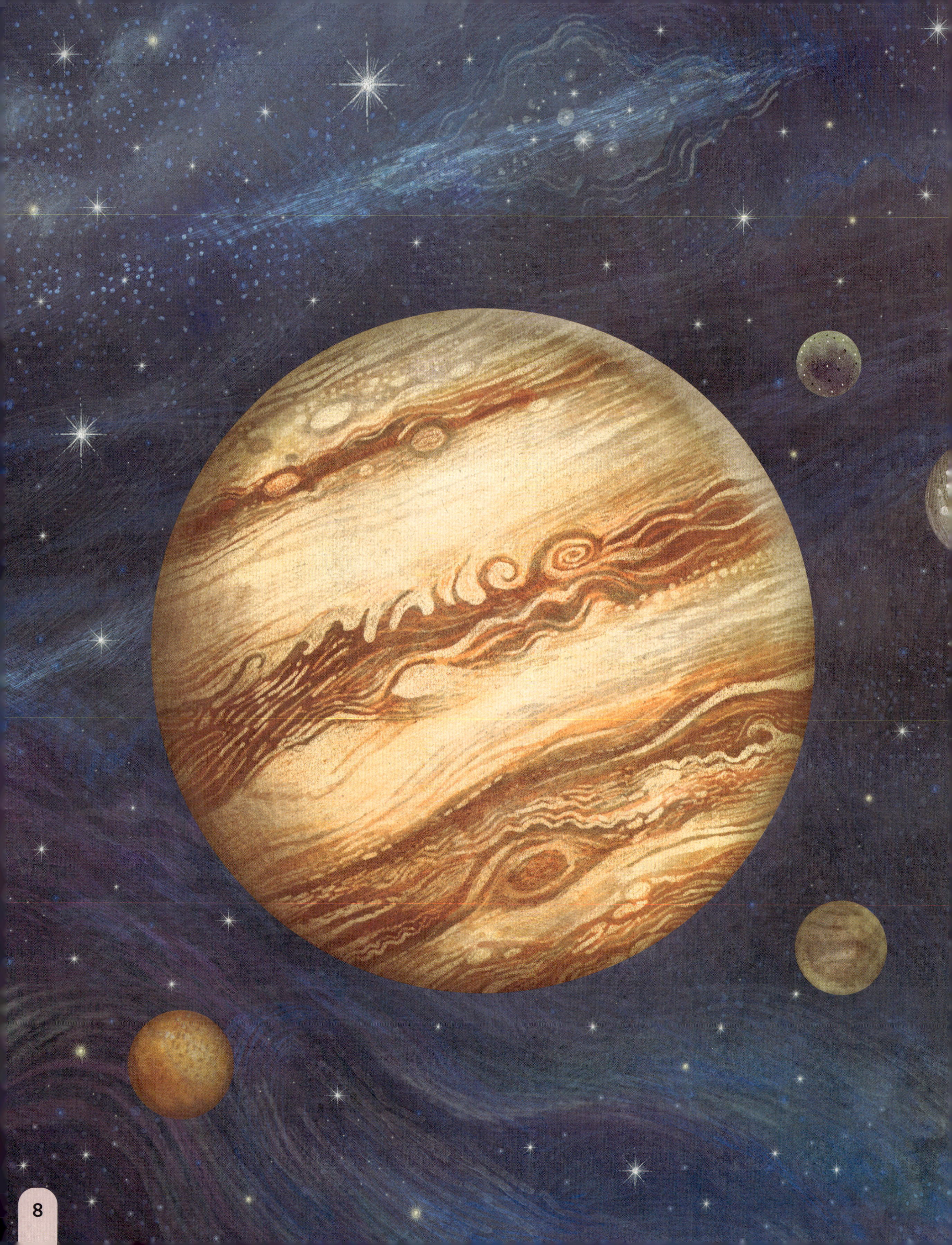

Amazing Space

For as long as humans have existed, we have been captivated by the starry night skies. In the past, people believed that unusual events like comets and eclipses foretold doom and disaster, glory in battle or the downfall of kings and emperors. Nowadays, we have a greater understanding of the science behind these rare astronomical oddities, yet we remain fascinated by them.

Blue Moons & Supermoons

The Moon, that beautiful glowing orb that hangs in the night sky above us, has always intrigued humans and fired our imaginations. You may have heard the phrase 'once in a blue moon' to describe something that happens rarely. But what exactly is a blue moon?

What is a Blue Moon?

A blue moon is not actually blue. Instead, the name 'blue moon' refers to a rare second full moon in any particular month. It takes the Moon roughly four weeks to circle the Earth, during which time it appears to go through different phases, from 'new' to 'full'. Normally, there are twelve full moons every year: one per month. But the Moon's cycle is actually 29.5 days, which is slightly shorter than the average month. This means that every two or three years, something special happens: we have a month that contains two full moons – one at the beginning of the month and one at the end. The second of these is known as a blue moon.

Although the name 'blue moon' doesn't normally refer to the Moon's colour, on rare occasions you might actually see a moon with a blue tinge. This is normally the result of particles of ash or dust in the atmosphere, from a forest fire or a volcanic eruption.

In 2018 there were two blue moons in just one year. The next time this will happen will be in 2037.

What is a Supermoon?

The Moon's orbit around the Earth isn't a perfect circle, so the distance between us and the Moon varies depending on where in its cycle it is. When a full moon appears while the Moon is closest to the Earth, the Moon looks bigger and brighter than normal – we call it a supermoon. This happens roughly three or four times a year. A 'super blue moon' is when the second full moon in a month comes when the Moon is at its closest point. On average, this rare event takes place only once every ten years or so.

Supermoon

Full Moon

A supermoon can look 14% larger and 30% brighter than the smallest full moon.

The Phases of the Moon

From Earth, the Moon appears to change shape slightly every night. This is because it orbits, or goes around, the Earth, and as it travels we see different amounts of its sunlit side.

11

Solar Eclipse

Picture a lovely sunny morning, with not a cloud in the sky. Then, imagine that suddenly, the light fades and darkness descends. The temperature drops. The birds fall silent. You look up and see a black disc obscuring the face of the Sun. A chill creeps across your skin, the hairs on your neck stand on end … This eerie, mysterious spectacle is something that only a small proportion of the world's population will ever experience: a total eclipse of the Sun.

The word 'eclipse' comes from the Greek for 'abandonment': in ancient times, people believed that the Sun was abandoning the Earth.

Omen of Disaster?

Long ago, people were often frightened by eclipses, seeing them as strange events that overturned the natural order of things. In ancient China, many believed that eclipses were caused by a giant dragon trying to swallow the Sun. In Mesopotamia, people thought that they foretold the death of the king. For the Inca people of South America, an eclipse that blotted out the life-giving Sun meant that the sun god was angry, so offerings and sacrifices were made to appease him.

Remember – never look directly at the Sun without special eye protection, because it can damage your eyes.

Shadow of the Moon

A solar eclipse is a rare sight. It happens when the Moon moves between the Earth and the Sun, blocking out the Sun's light and casting a shadow on Earth. When the Moon completely covers the Sun, this is known as a total solar eclipse. It can be seen from only a small region of the Earth's surface at a time, for only a few minutes – you have to be in the right place at the right time to experience it.

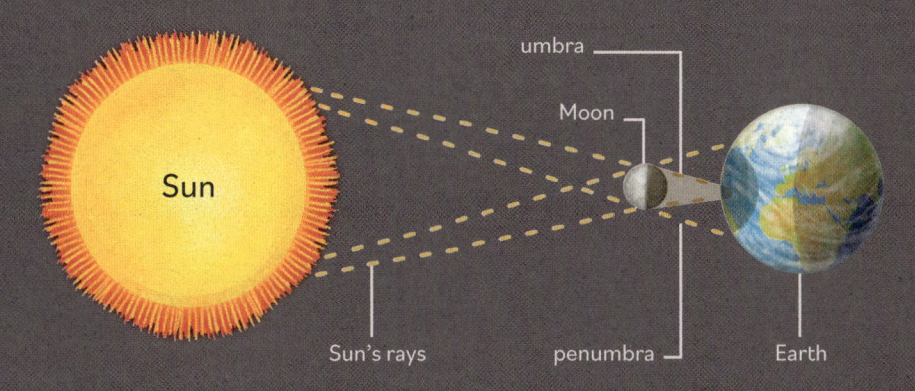

The dark centre of the Moon's shadow is called the umbra; the outer part is the penumbra. In the small area where the umbra falls, the entire Sun will be blocked out. In the penumbra, part of the Sun will remain visible – this is called a partial eclipse. In a partial eclipse, it looks as if a bite has been taken out of the Sun. In a total eclipse, a glowing halo might be visible around the blacked-out Sun. This is known as the 'corona' (Latin for 'crown').

Partial Solar Eclipse

Because the Moon circles the Earth every month, you might think it would block out the Sun more often. But it orbits at an angle, so it only lines up to create a solar eclipse occasionally.

Total Solar Eclipse

A total solar eclipse happens somewhere on our planet roughly every 18 months. But a particular spot on Earth will experience a total eclipse only once every three or four hundred years!

Halley's Comet

Since ancient times, people have watched the heavens at night and wondered about the objects moving among them. Long ago, the rare appearance of a comet in the sky, with its dramatic trailing tail of light, was often seen as a portent of doom ...

Historic Sightings

One of the most famous comets – Halley's Comet – can be seen from Earth only every 75 years or so. Its appearance throughout human history can be traced back more than two thousand years to ancient Greece and China. In 1066, the comet's appearance was blamed for the English defeat at the Battle of Hastings. Its fly-by in 1222, streaking westwards through the skies, is said to have inspired the Mongol warrior Genghis Khan to conquer the lands to the west. At the time, these sightings were believed to be isolated events – nobody realised what they had in common.

Halley's Discovery

It wasn't until 1705 that the astronomer Edmond Halley worked out what was going on. He studied reports of sightings from 1531, 1607 and 1682, and he realised that they were not separate events – they were actually the same comet, returning again and again every 75 years. He predicted that it would be back in 1758, but he didn't live long enough to see himself proved right. Sure enough, the comet was spotted in December that year, and was named in Halley's honour.

The word 'comet' comes from the Ancient Greek kometes, meaning 'long-haired', referring to the streaming tail.

The solid centre, or nucleus, of Halley's Comet was photographed by the Giotto spacecraft in 1986. It is believed to measure roughly 15 kilometres long by 8 kilometres wide.

What is a Comet?

A comet, sometimes called a dirty snowball, is a block of ice and dust that orbits the Sun, reflecting its light. As it draws close to the Sun, the ice begins to melt, sending spectacular tails of gas and dust streaking out behind it, sometimes for millions of miles.

The last time Halley's Comet was seen from Earth was in 1986. It will not return to our skies until 2061.

The Transit of Venus

Another extremely rare stargazing event occurs when the planet Venus can be seen passing directly across the bright face of the Sun, like a small shadow. Venus, the Earth and the Sun line up roughly every 584 days, but the path of Venus, as seen from Earth, usually passes above or below the Sun, not across the face of it. Since the telescope was invented in 1610, this special event has happened only seven times. The last time was in 2012. It won't happen again until the year 2117!

Tunguska Fireball

On June 30th 1908, in a remote region of Siberia in Russia, a mysterious event took place near the Tunguska River. That morning, an enormous explosion ripped the sky apart, tearing through a huge area of forest and flattening millions of trees.
For decades after, nobody knew what had caused this strange explosion …
If it was a meteorite from space, where was the impact crater?

The Tunguska Puzzle

Because the region was so remote, scientists didn't investigate the scene until nearly twenty years later. They found a vast area of scorched and flattened trees, along with the bones of hundreds of dead reindeer. Local people described seeing a large fireball hurtling across the sky, followed by a flash of light, a pillar of flame and a booming sound like cannon-fire. It was powerful enough to knock people off their feet and shatter windows 60 kilometres away. Scientists suspected the culprit could have been a meteorite (a rock from space), but there was no sign of a crater where it landed. It was a mystery.

This mysterious event caused strange glowing skies across Europe for several weeks. In the UK, more than 5,000 kilometres away, the skies on the night of July 1st were said to have been bright enough to read by.

The Tunguska explosion was so powerful that it could be heard 1,000 kilometres away.

Mystery Solved?

Today, scientists still argue about exactly what happened, but many think the explosion was caused by a space rock about the size of a 25-storey building rushing through the atmosphere at about 54,000 kilometres per hour (twenty times the speed of a fighter jet). This staggering speed would have compressed the air in front of the rock, creating immense temperatures that caused it to explode about 5 kilometres above the Earth's surface. This is what is known as a meteor air burst.

In 2013, there was another, smaller meteor air burst above Chelyabinsk, Russia. The blast broke windows and injured more than a thousand people. Studying this explosion helped experts work out what may have happened at Tunguska.

Too Close For Comfort

Fortunately, the Tunguska event took place where few people lived – it is thought that although 80 million trees were destroyed in an area the size of a large city, only two people died. Luckily, events like this are very rare. Scientists estimate that there probably won't be another object of such a destructive size hurtling our way for another thousand years or so. In the meantime, they are working on a defence system that aims to use rockets to nudge dangerous comets or asteroids off course.

Supernova

One of the rarest and most spectacular events that can be spotted by stargazers is a supernova: a colossal explosion that occurs when a huge star reaches the end of its life, going out in a blaze of glory.

The Life Cycle of A Star

A star is an enormous burning ball of hydrogen and helium gas. Most stars burn brightly for millions – or even billions – of years. At the end of a star's life, when it runs out of fuel, its size determines what happens next. A small star will quietly fade away, but a big one makes a dramatic exit.

In our galaxy, the Milky Way, a supernova explodes roughly every fifty years, but we can't see most of them because they are obscured by space dust. The last time a supernova was spotted in the Milky Way was in 1604, but powerful telescopes help astronomers see supernovas in nearby galaxies.

Star Wars

Usually, there are two opposing forces at work on a star: pressure and gravity. A star burns huge amounts of fuel in its core, which produces extreme heat, causing a pressure that pushes outwards. Meanwhile, gravity – the force that pulls things towards each other – is also at work, squeezing the star inwards. For most of a star's life, this inward squeeze from gravity is balanced by the outward pressure. But when a massive star runs out of fuel, the core cools and the pressure drops. Then, gravity wins the battle and the whole star collapses in on itself in seconds, setting off a jaw-droppingly enormous explosion that sends shockwaves rippling across the galaxy.

Black Hole

After the outer layers of a star have been thrown off by the explosion, the collapsed core may become a black hole: a strange, dense object whose gravity is so strong that it sucks everything towards it. Even light can't escape a black hole's powerful pull, so this mysterious object is invisible against the inky darkness of space.

Most stars are not big enough to become supernovas: only stars more than eight times heavier than the Sun have a chance of ending this way.

The explosion can be brighter than a billion Suns. Although the main blast lasts only a few seconds, the afterglow remains for several months.

The outer layers, which explode into space, will become part of the next generation of stars and planets. Did you know, even humans are made of star dust? Every human contains some elements made billions of years ago by an exploding star!

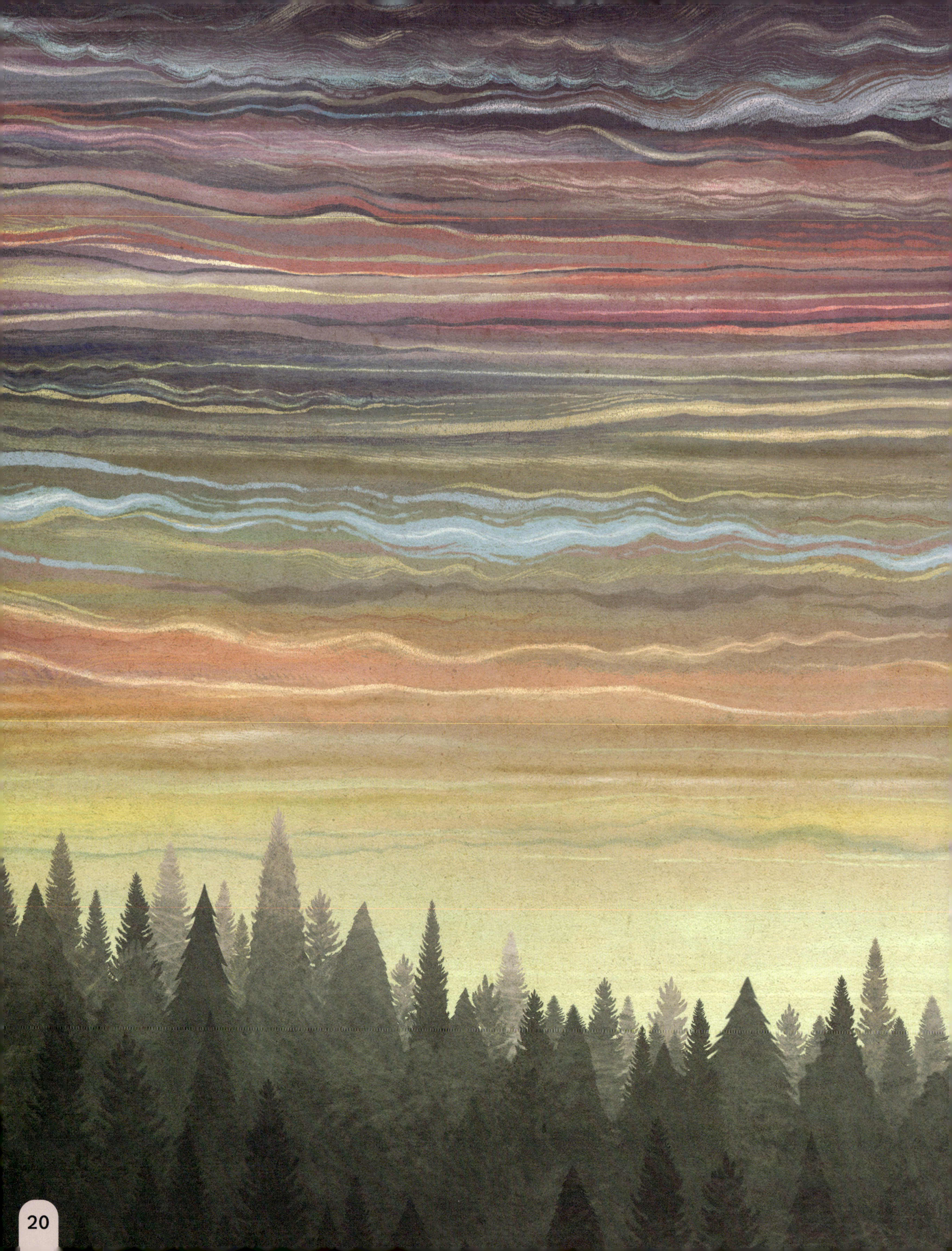

Weird Weather

The powerful forces of the weather bring about some of nature's most awe-inspiring phenomena. In the outer edges of the atmosphere, the solar wind stirs up stunning light shows. Lower down, as the sun's rays pass through icy clouds, they conjure unusual rainbows, mock suns and other puzzling illusions. As storms rage, they produce bizarre balls of light, or strange blue flames that flicker from masts or flag poles. Our ever-changing skies are full of wonders.

Nature's Light Show

One of nature's most spectacular displays takes place in the northern and southern skies, around the poles. Far above the Earth, high-energy particles that have travelled all the way from the Sun collide with gases in the atmosphere to paint the sky green, red and violet, creating a beautiful light show that ripples across the heavens.

Dance of the Solar Winds

Auroras are caused when solar winds carry highly charged particles from the Sun towards Earth. They collide with Earth's magnetic field, which acts like a protective forcefield. Most of the particles are deflected, but some become trapped in the magnetic field and are funnelled down towards the poles. They crash into gas molecules in the atmosphere, making the molecules glow, which causes swirling lights in the sky. The colours depend on which gases the solar particles bump into: oxygen creates red or green lights; nitrogen produces blues and purples.

The Northern Lights are called the Aurora Borealis, and the Southern Lights are the Aurora Australis. They are named after Aurora, Roman goddess of the dawn.

It is rarer to see the Southern Lights than the Northern Lights, because there are fewer accessible landmasses in the southern hemisphere to see them from.

Rare Sightings

Close to the poles, in places such as Norway and Alaska, the aurora is visible for much of the year – but further away, it is rarer. When there are storms on the Sun's surface, the solar winds become more forceful. Every eleven years or so, when the solar wind is particularly strong, auroras can be seen across a wide area. The year 1859 saw the most intense solar storm in recorded history, causing spectacular auroras across the globe. At 1 a.m. on September 1st, the glow over the Rocky Mountains was so bright that gold miners woke up and began having breakfast, believing it was morning. In Cuba, the skies were so red they appeared stained with blood.

A brilliant aurora in England in 1938 resulted in the fire brigade being called to Windsor Castle, because people thought it was burning!

The Roaring Aurora

Sometimes, strange crackling and whooshing sounds seem to accompany the aurora. But for years, scientists dismissed the idea of the aurora making noises, saying that because the lights are created more than 100 kilometres above the ground, any sounds would be out of earshot. However, in 2022 scientists set up recording equipment in a Finnish village, and found that about 5 per cent of the strongest auroras were joined by a chorus of whistles and cracks. It's thought that the auroras cause sparks of electrical energy in the atmosphere, which produce these sounds.

Sun Dogs & Moonbows

Long ago, people were often awestruck by the strange and beautiful things they saw in the sky. Glowing haloes, colourful arcs and mysterious extra suns were sometimes thought to be signs from the gods. Nowadays, we understand that these natural wonders are caused by light bending as it travels through water droplets or ice crystals in the air. They continue to fascinate us, just as they captivated the people of the past.

The official name for sun dogs is 'parhelia', which is Greek for 'beside the Sun'.

For centuries, people have linked sun dogs with impending wet weather. This is backed up by the science: the icy clouds that cause sun dogs often appear before rain.

As well as sun dogs, there are also moon dogs: bright patches either side of the Moon.

Mock Suns

On a bright winter's day, strange optical illusions can occur, such as sun dogs: patches of light that appear beside the Sun, like dogs flanking their master. Sun dogs, or mock suns, are caused by sunlight bending as it passes through horizontal ice crystals in the atmosphere. They can sometimes be seen on cold days when the Sun is low in the sky.

Three Sons of York

During the English Wars of the Roses, the appearance of sun dogs played a part in shaping history. As dawn broke on 2nd February 1461, two armies prepared for battle. The soon-to-be king, Edward IV, convinced his soldiers that the three suns they could see rising in the sky foretold glory for the three sons of the House of York (Edward and his brothers). He claimed it was a sign of God's favour, and he went on to win the battle – and the throne.

Be careful – looking directly at the Sun can damage your eyes.

What is a Moonbow?

A rainbow appears when sunlight splits into separate colours as it passes through raindrops. A moonbow is rarer. This special type of rainbow appears by the light of the Moon, when the conditions are just right. If you look towards the rain or the mist from a waterfall when there's a full moon hanging low in the sky behind you (just before dawn or after sunset), you might be lucky enough to see one.

St Elmo's Fire

For centuries, sailors navigating the seas reported something strange. During storms, they sometimes noticed ghostly blue lights flickering around the tops of their ships' masts. This eerie glow looked like fire, but did not burn. These puzzling flames remained a mystery until the 1750s, when American scientist Benjamin Franklin worked out that they were caused by electricity.

St Elmo's Fire is named after the patron saint of sailors (also known as St Erasmus).

Electricity In the Air

St Elmo's Fire is the name for the rare flickering lights that sometimes form around tall objects during a thunderstorm. This strange phenomenon is not fire, and it's not lightning - it's a highly charged gas called plasma. In a storm, the atmosphere becomes charged with electrical energy. It gathers around tall structures, transforming the gas molecules in the air into glowing plasma that fizzes and hisses, sometimes lasting for several minutes.

In the past, sailors saw the appearance of these blue flames as a good omen, as if the protective hand of Saint Elmo was guiding them through a storm.

Standing Tall

The lights of St Elmo's Fire do not only happen at sea. They can also be seen around church spires, flag poles, weather vanes, and other tall, pointed objects. These glowing lights sometimes cling to aircraft in flight, dancing around the wingtips or propellers.

OCEAN ODDITIES

Aside from St Elmo's Fire, other strange weather phenomena can happen at sea.

Fair-Weather Waterspout

These spinning columns of air and water appear above lakes and oceans, forming at the surface and reaching skywards. They last for up to twenty minutes, and can extend over 100 metres high.

Green Flash

This elusive wonder sometimes happens at sunset, when the atmosphere bends and scatters the light, leaving a fleeting flash of green as the sun disappears beneath the horizon. It's a rare sight that is only visible occasionally, when the sky is very clear.

Fata Morgana

Named after King Arthur's sorceress sister, this rare type of mirage transforms distant objects, such as boats or islands, creating strange visions of ships or cities that seem to float in the air. These illusions occur when light rays are bent by layers of warm and cool air, which sometimes form above the ocean.

Ball Lightning

Ever since humans have existed, we have been amazed and terrified by the dazzling, destructive power of lightning. These days, we understand that lightning happens when bolts of electricity jump from the clouds to the ground. But there is a different kind of lightning – a rare and mysterious natural wonder that has baffled scientists for centuries: ball lightning.

Some say that sightings of ball lightning are responsible for many reports of UFOs.

A globe of ball lightning lasts for about 25 seconds, on average.

What Is It?

Since ancient times, people have reported seeing floating balls of light, often during or just after a lightning storm. Unlike a speedy flash of lightning, these glowing orbs usually last for several seconds. There are many different descriptions of ball lightning: it can range from the size of a pea to the size of a small car; it may appear in many different colours; it may fizzle out quietly, or explode with a bang. It has even been known to enter buildings through chimneys and closed windows!

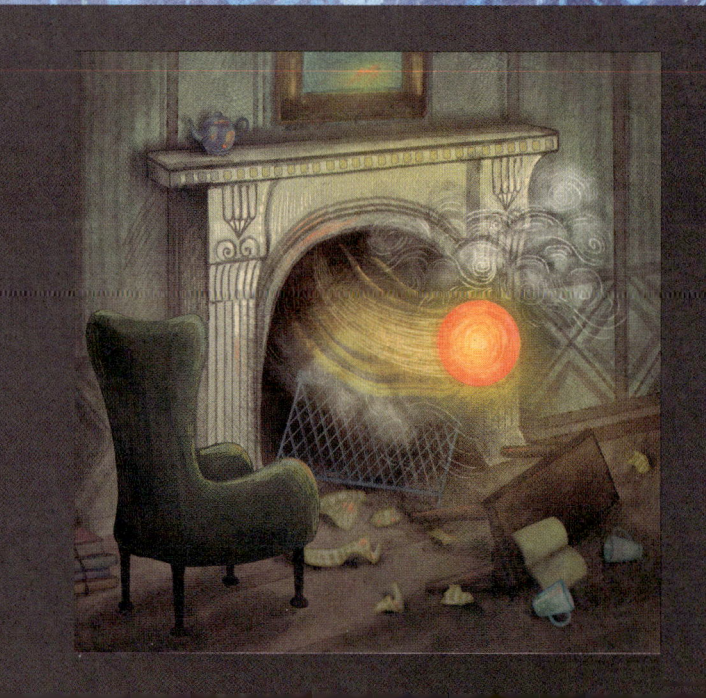

Not all ball lightning is the same – different types may have different causes.

What Causes It?

Scientists can't say for certain what causes ball lightning – there are lots of different theories. Some say these glowing orbs are balls of hot, highly charged gas called plasma, created when the air is super-heated by lightning. Others say it happens when a substance in the soil, called silicon, is vaporized by a lightning strike and becomes a kind of floating, glowing cloud. Another idea is that ball lightning is a type of microwave radiation, which would explain why it can move through glass. Because ball lightning is so rare and unpredictable, it is very difficult to study, so it may continue to puzzle scientists for years to come.

According to an investigation carried out by an American scientist in 1960, ball lightning has been seen by about 5% of the world's population.

Who's Seen It?

Throughout history, many people have reported seeing this strange phenomenon. In 1638, a 'great ball of fire' is said to have barrelled into an English church, smashing pews and windows and giving off a thick, dark smoke. When he was a child in the 1870s, the future Russian tsar Nicholas II was terrified by a fiery ball that came through a chapel window. In 1907, ball lighting apparently destroyed a lighthouse in Australia, and in 1963 a scientist saw a glowing sphere moving along the aisle of a passenger plane flying from New York to Washington during a storm.

Curious Clouds

Always changing and shape-shifting, clouds are the everyday wonders of our skies – but some types are much less common than others. These remarkable cloud formations are among the most unusual and fascinating.

Lenticular Clouds

If you're in the mountains and you see what looks like a flying saucer, it's probably a lenticular cloud. These spectacular, disc-shaped clouds can appear near mountain peaks, sometimes piling up in layers like a stack of pancakes. They are formed when moist air is blocked by a large obstacle – such as a mountain – and is forced upwards, where the water vapour cools and condenses into a saucer-shaped cloud. Most impressive at sunset, lenticular clouds are often tinged with pastel hues, reflecting the colours of the setting sun.

Looking similar to a hovering saucer, a lenticular cloud could easily be mistaken for a UFO.

The most impressive lenticular clouds form around solitary mountain peaks, such as Mount Fuji in Japan.

Morning Glory

Off the northern coast of Queensland, Australia, a huge, long tube of cloud occasionally appears, sweeping in from the sea like a rolling wave. These rare clouds - called Morning Glories - form over the ocean at night when cool air blowing towards the land slips under layers of warm air to create a spinning roll. They can sometimes stretch for over 1,000 kilometres (the same length as Great Britain)!

Nacreous Clouds

These rare, very high clouds are only visible in polar regions when the air is dry and the sun has dropped below the horizon. Crystals of ice inside the clouds scatter the fading light, which makes the clouds shimmer in pearly colours when lit from below.

Billow Clouds

Resembling swirls of icing on a cake, these extremely rare clouds look like the crests of ocean waves. They form when two layers of air blow at different speeds, the upper stream blowing faster, whipping the clouds into billowing peaks.

Strange Snow

If you've ever seen a snow crystal up close, you'll know that each one is a little miracle – a tiny, intricate wonder of nature. Of course, snow itself is not particularly rare, but there are some snowy sights that are so unusual they have become the stuff of winter legends.

Giant Snowballs

One morning in 2016, local people from the village of Nyda, on the Arctic coast of Siberia, were amazed to discover thousands of enormous snowballs clustered on the shoreline. These icy globes, ranging from the width of a tennis ball to the size of a large beach ball, are very unusual. They are thought to have formed when pieces of ice were rolled around in a particular way by the movement of the wind and tide. Similar giant snowballs also appeared in Finland in 2014, and on the shores of Lake Michigan, USA, in 2015.

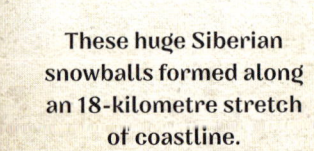

These huge Siberian snowballs formed along an 18-kilometre stretch of coastline.

Snow Rollers

Sometimes measuring more than half a metre wide, these strange snowy doughnuts only appear under certain rare conditions. They are made when the wind blows across a snow-covered hillside or field. There must be a thick layer of snow that is not too tightly packed, and the wind must be brisk but not too strong. The temperature has to be just right so the snow is sticky, not hard or slushy.

Giant Snowflakes

Snowflakes are made up of lots of tiny snow crystals clustered together. They are normally about a centimetre wide, but in 1887, 38-centimetre clusters fell on Montana, USA – that's bigger than a flying disc! Giant snowflake clusters only form when the temperature hovers just above freezing and the winds are light, so the clumps don't break up.

Watermelon Snow

Snow is normally white or tinged with blue, but watermelon snow is pink! Sometimes, in polar regions or in the mountains, when the snow begins to melt during warmer weather, the snow takes on the reddish colour of a type of algae that lies beneath it.

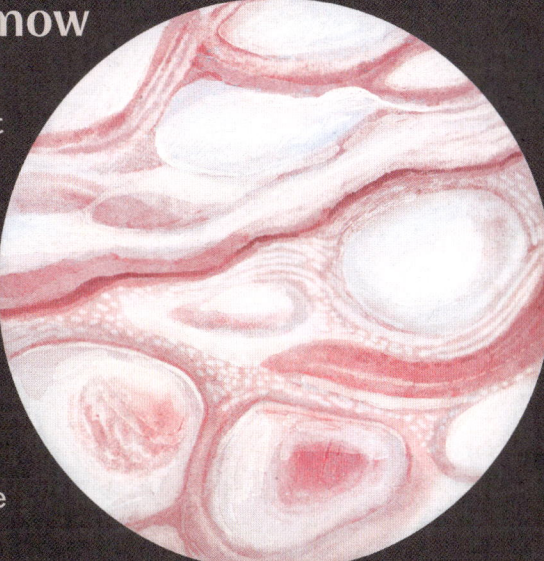

Peculiar Plants

In a small Mexican town stands a tree with a trunk so wide that it takes thirty children, arms outstretched, to encircle it. On a remote island in the Indian Ocean grows an unusual kind of tree that weeps a blood-like resin when wounded. In the jungles of Borneo lives a rare plant that feeds on lizards and rats. From the biggest, smelliest flowers on the planet to ghostly fungi that glow in the dark, the world of unusual plants is remarkable in its richness and variety.

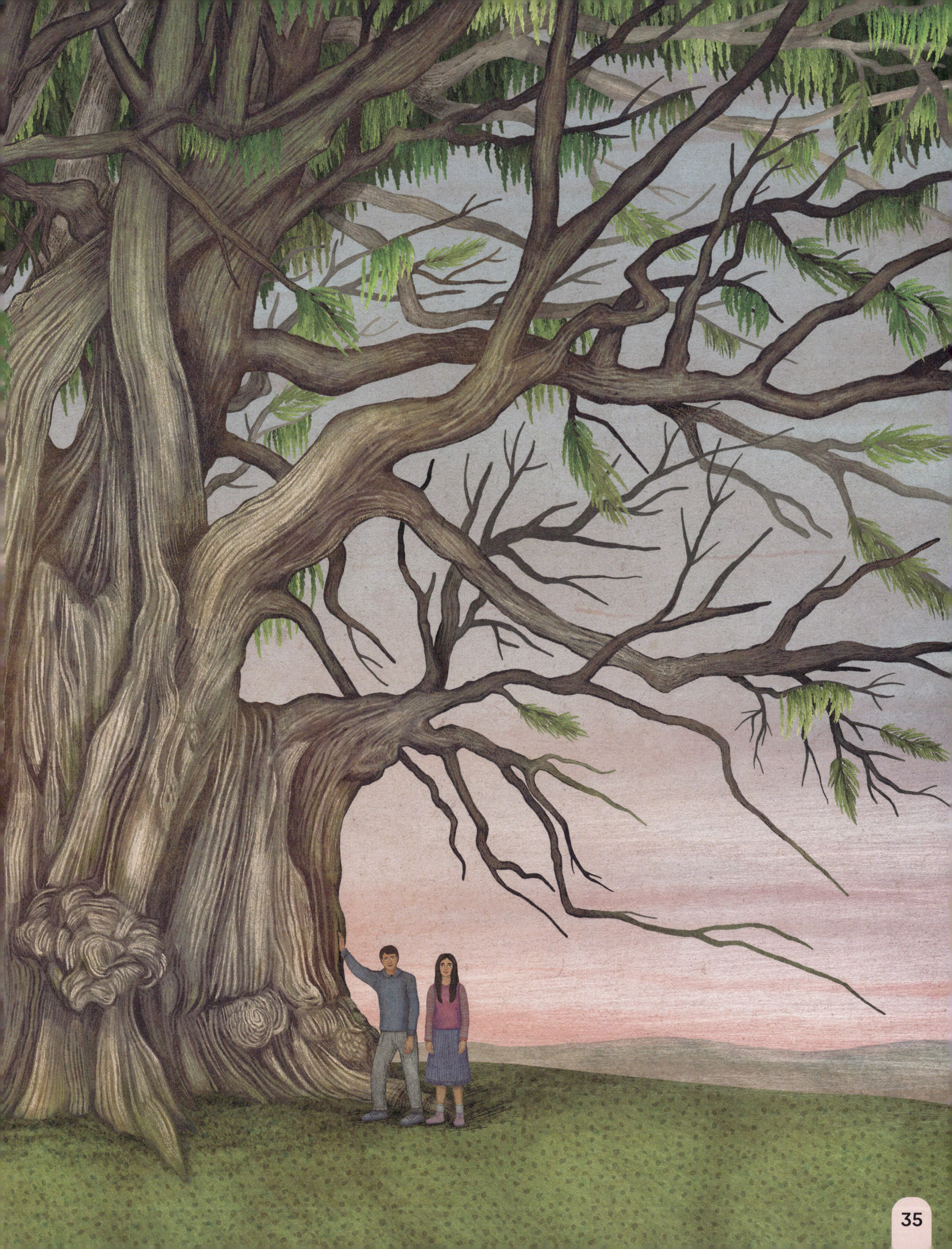

Rare Blooming Flowers

Sometimes, nature guards its secrets closely. There are a few plants that bloom so rarely that to witness their flowering feels like stumbling upon treasure. These are the hidden jewels of the natural world . . .

The Queen of the Night

Just once a year, on a midsummer night, a magical event takes place amid the craggy canyons of North America's Sonoran Desert: the flowering of the night-blooming cereus. This cactus is the Cinderella of the plant world. For most of the year, its gangly stems look like a collection of dry twigs . . . but for one night between May and July, its buds unfurl to reveal beautiful, fragrant flowers whose delicate petals glow gently in the moonlight. By the time the sun rises the next day, these spectacular, saucer-sized blooms will have withered away, almost as if they were never there at all.

Making a beautiful flower is hard work. Having flowers that bloom for just one night a year helps the cereus conserve its energy.

Why does the cereus bloom at night? Because this is when hawk moths are active, and the plant relies on these insects to pollinate its flowers.

Although each flower blooms only once per year, a cereus plant may produce several different flowers that open over the course of a few nights.

In the darkness, a hawk moth flits between flowers, lured by the rich, sweet nectar, which it sips through a tubelike tongue.

Kurinji Blossoms

Once every 12 years, certain hillsides in the Western Ghats mountains of southwest India become blanketed in purple flowers. They all bloom at the same time to lessen the risk that their seeds, when they form, will be eaten by birds and other wildlife. It's nature's way of helping the plant survive.

Palmer's Agave

This plant, which grows in the deserts of Mexico and the southwest USA, can live for up to 25 years. During its lifetime it will flower only once, just before it dies. Some types of bat, which feed on nectar, time their migrations to tie in with the blooming of these special flowers.

Queen of the Andes

High in the mountains of Peru and Bolivia lives a very rare plant that blooms only once in its 100-year lifetime! But when it flowers, it really flowers – a single plant can produce thousands of tiny blooms on a towering stem, which can reach up to 15 metres tall. These flowers last for just a few weeks before the plant dies.

Green Giants

Rooted in the earth but reaching for the skies, trees clean the air and produce oxygen, as well as providing food and homes for countless creatures. While all trees are remarkable, some are particularly extraordinary, and these impressive examples are the record-breakers of the woodland world.

Big Banyan

The Thimmamma banyan in southeast India has the largest canopy of any tree on Earth, sprawling across more than 5 acres – about the same area as three football pitches. This ancient giant is a strangler fig. About 550 years ago, its seed would have landed among the branches of another tree. The young sprout sent its vinelike roots down to the ground to soak up water and nutrients. These roots eventually thickened into woody pillars, smothering the original tree by robbing it of sunlight and nutrients. It is still growing today, spreading its roots and branches in every direction.

Tallest Tree

Standing proud in California's Redwood National Park is Hyperion, the tallest tree on the planet. This coast redwood measures just over 116 metres: 20 metres taller than London's Big Ben tower. Hyperion is believed to be between 600 and 800 years old . . . and it's still growing.

Widest Trunk

The Árbol del Tule, a Montezuma cypress rooted inside a churchyard in Oaxaca, Mexico, has an astonishingly thick trunk. It measures 36 metres around, and 14 metres in diameter at its widest point. It takes about thirty children, holding hands, to encircle this 1,500-year-old giant.

Beneath the canopy is a temple where pilgrims offer prayers to the Hindu goddess Ammavaru.

The enormous canopy of this ancient, sacred tree is supported by more than 4,000 prop roots.

Biggest by Volume

With a circumference of 31 metres at the base and a height of more than 83 metres, General Sherman - a giant sequoia growing in California's Sierra Nevada mountains - is the biggest tree in the world.

Oldest Living Tree

Methuselah, a bristlecone pine from the White Mountains of California, began life 4,850 years ago, before the Egyptian pyramids were built! To date it, scientists took a sample from its core. An even more ancient bristlecone pine, over 5,000 years old, has been discovered, but its location is being kept secret for the tree's protection.

Bleeding Trees

If a tree is cut or damaged, it will often release a thick, sticky liquid, called resin, to cover the wound and protect itself. Often, this resin is a golden colour, but some rare trees ooze a deep-red liquid that looks remarkably like blood. Many myths have grown up around these marvels of nature.

Dragon's Blood Tree

Among the rugged landscapes of Socotra – a remote island in the Indian Ocean – live many peculiar plants and animals. The bizarre-looking dragon's blood tree is astonishing not only for its otherworldly appearance and its centuries-long lifespan, but also because it bleeds a crimson resin if injured.

People harvest the trees' precious, blood-red resin, known as dragon's blood, for use in medicines, varnishes and dyes.

Dragon's blood trees face many threats, including free-roaming goats that feed on the young saplings, as well as droughts and cyclones brought on by the changing climate.

40

It's tricky to calculate the age of these slow-growing trees, because they have no growth rings in their trunks. However, it's thought they can live for more than a thousand years.

According to legend, the first of these trees sprang up from the blood of a dying dragon!

The branches reach skywards, like an upturned umbrella, to collect moisture from the air.

Bleeding Yew

St Brynach's churchyard in Nevern, Wales, is home to an ancient avenue of gnarled and twisted yews. One is famous for the blood-like liquid that has oozed from its trunk for as long as anyone can remember. Some say it bleeds because an innocent man was hanged from its branches centuries ago. Others say the 'blood' is escaping rainwater, stained red by the tree's heartwood.

Bloodwood Tree

The sawn-off logs of the African bloodwood tree look like something from a horror film. When the tree is wounded, it seeps a dark-red resin from beneath the bark. These trees – valued for their timber and their precious resin – are at risk from over-harvesting and are now a protected species.

Sangre de Drago

Growing in Peru, Ecuador and other parts of South America, the Sangre de Drago (Dragon's Blood) tree produces a thick, red, bloodlike resin. This natural antiseptic is highly prized by local people as a liquid bandage to treat wounds.

Carnivorous Plants

Some extraordinary plants manage to thrive in places where the soil is low in nutrients. To survive, they have developed curious ways of boosting their diets . . . by trapping and eating animals! Most carnivorous plants grow only in very specific parts of the world, so seeing them in the wild is a special event.

Attenborough's Pitcher Plant

Named after the beloved British naturalist Sir David Attenborough, this extraordinary shrub only grows on a few remote mountain slopes on the island of Palawan in the Philippines. It is a type of pitcher plant, whose large leaves form jug-shaped traps. When small creatures come to sip the sweet nectar from the rim of the slippery trap, they often fall into the pitcher. Inside is a soup of digestive juices where the creatures slowly dissolve, their nutrients absorbed by the plant.

As well as catching insects, this plant is large enough to snare small mammals, such as shrews.

The traps of Attenborough's pitcher plant can measure up to 30 centimetres tall and can hold about 1.5 litres of acidic liquid.

This plant is critically endangered – there are only a few hundred of them left in the wild.

Monkey Cup

This endangered species, also known as the giant Malaysian pitcher plant, grows only in a small region of Borneo. It is possibly the biggest meat-eating plant on the planet, with pitchers up to 41 centimetres tall, able to digest frogs, lizards, birds and rats as well as insects. It also feeds on the droppings of shrews and other rodents, who plop them into the pitchers as they feed on nectar from the lid.

Venus Flytrap

Common in garden centres but rare in the wild, the Venus flytrap is found only in a few small wetland regions of North and South Carolina, USA. If an insect brushes against the hairy leaves, they snap shut, then slowly digest the victim. It is one of very few plants that can move quickly, closing its traps in less than half a second.

King Sundew

When an insect lands on a sundew, or 'flypaper plant', it gets stuck to the sweet-smelling, glue-covered tentacles. Then, the leaf folds over to ensnare and digest the prey. One of the largest sundew plants, the king sundew, is extremely rare in the wild, growing only in a single valley in South Africa.

Extraordinary Flowers

The mountainous rainforests of Sumatra, in Indonesia, are home to some of the rarest and most peculiar flowers on the planet. Not only are the titan arum and the giant padma two of the largest flowers on Earth, they are also two of the stinkiest! Both have been given the name 'corpse flower' because of their disgusting smell.

Titan Arum

Described as the worst-smelling flower in the world, the titan arum has an aroma similar to rotting flesh. Seeing – or smelling – this unique flower is no easy feat, because it blooms only once every five to ten years. On the rare nights when it flowers, the plant heats up, helping waft its putrid scent far and wide. The smell, which can be detected from half a mile away, attracts flies and carrion beetles to pollinate the plant.

The bloom can reach up to 3 metres tall, growing 15 centimetres per day. After one or two days in flower, it collapses.

It can take many years for the titan arum to store up the energy it needs to produce such a big bloom.

Technically, the titan arum is not a single flower, but a group of little flowers gathered together on a central spike called a spadix.

Fewer than 1,000 of these remarkable plants are thought to be left in the wild.

Giant Padma

The largest flower in the world, the giant padma, or Rafflesia, measures about a metre across and smells of rotting meat. Remarkable not only for its huge flower and its foul smell, the giant padma is extra unusual in that it has no roots, no stem and no leaves. For most of its life cycle this rare plant is largely invisible, hidden inside a jungle vine, sucking up food and water from its host. Eventually, the buds break through the bark of the host vine like little cabbages. The flowers bloom once a year, but last for only a few days before shrivelling away.

Glowing Fungi

Foxfire. Fairy sparks. Torchwood... These are names for the strange, glowing lights that people across the world have sometimes noticed in the woods at night. Produced by luminous fungi, these elusive, eerie lights have sparked curiosity and wonder through the ages.

Ancient Mystery

More than 2,300 years ago, the ancient Greek writer Aristotle described the 'cold fire' given off by 'glowing wood', but for centuries people were baffled by the cause of these strange lights. It wasn't until the nineteenth century, when glowing wooden props from German coal mines were examined, that scientists realised the lights were caused by fungi growing on the wood. The glow is thanks to a chemical reaction – the same trick fireflies use to light up their tails on a summer night.

Foxfire

Foxfire is the name of the glow caused when a fungus inside a rotting log illuminates the wood.

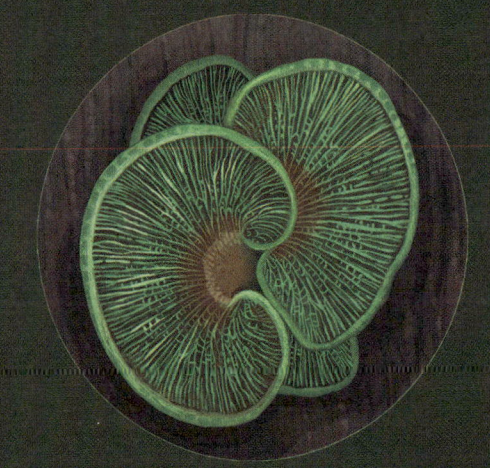

Bitter Oyster

The glow from this type of fungus, which grows in clumps on tree trunks, is often bright enough to read by.

Jack O'Lantern

Orange by day, the feathery gills of this poisonous mushroom glow a ghostly green colour by night.

The word 'bioluminescent', meaning 'living light', describes animals and plants that produce their own light through chemical reactions.

Why Glow?

There are several possible reasons why fungi put on such magical displays. Perhaps they glow to attract pollinators (beetles and other insects) who spread their spores far and wide, helping them reproduce. Some mushrooms might glow as a warning, deterring creatures from eating their poisonous flesh. Or perhaps the lights are a side-effect of the process fungi use to break down dead wood.

In the 1600s, a Dutch botanist described how people from Ambon Island in Indonesia used glowing fungi as torches.

Some Australian mushrooms, including this type (Mycena lampadis) from Queensland, are particularly luminous.

Only a small fraction of fungi have this superpower. Out of the 150,000 fungi species discovered so far, only about 100 of these glow in the dark.

Green Pepe

This tiny toadstool, which grows on rotting logs in damp forests, is known in Japan as yakoh-také: the 'night-light' mushroom.

Ghost Fungus

Lighting up the forest floor with its dramatic light, the ghost fungus is a special sight in southern Australia.

47

Unusual Animals

Sometimes the natural world is truly surprising. In 1938, a wildlife photographer in Kenya was stunned when he spotted a peculiar white giraffe that stood out from its companions. On a foggy day in 1947, thousands of fish started to rain down on a small town in the USA. In 2005, hundreds of toads that lived in a pond in Germany began exploding, with no obvious cause. In this chapter, we will explore the extraordinary – and sometimes surreal – stories of some of nature's most unusual animals.

49

Raining Fish & Frogs

Imagine you're walking along, when suddenly – thump, thump, splat! – hundreds of frogs start dropping from the sky all around you, their slippery bodies sliding down car windscreens and piling up on the pavement. It sounds like something from a strange dream, but this bizarre phenomenon is something that actually happens – just very rarely.

It never really rains cats and dogs – but it does rain fish and frogs. However, these peculiar events are very rare.

Strange Tales

Since ancient times, there have been accounts of frogs, fish and other flightless creatures falling from the heavens. In 1794, French soldiers sheltering in a trench outside the village of Lalain, near Lille, were pelted by a mysterious rain of tiny toads, which got caught in the rims of their three-cornered hats. Scotland in the 1800s saw several unexplained showers of herring. One morning in 1947 in Marksville, USA, thousands of fish began falling from the sky, landing on roofs, piling up in trucks, and striking people on the head as they walked to work.

Fishy Funnel

Scientists think these strange showers are probably caused by strong storms, tornadoes and whirling waterspouts, which – very occasionally – suck up fish or other creatures from the surface of the ocean or a lake. These unusual passengers are whisked across the sky for a while, then dropped to earth as the wind dies down.

In June 2005, thousands of living frogs rained from the sky in Odžaci, Serbia.

The small town of Lajamanu, Australia, was showered in falling fish not only in February 2023, but also in 2010, 2004 and in 1974.

Frog Hail

One day in 1882, in Dubuque, Iowa, USA, huge hailstones containing live frogs fell from the skies. As soon as the ice melted, the frogs hopped away.

Worm Shower

On a summer day in 2007 in Jennings, Louisiana, USA, a woman crossing the road noticed large clumps of worms raining down around her.

Torrential Tadpoles

In June 2009 in Ishikawa, Japan, thousands of tadpoles showered onto roofs, gardens and car windscreens.

Uncommon Creatures

Sometimes in nature, a rare, very special creature appears that is a blend of two separate species. Normally, animals from different species can't have babies together – but in some unusual cases, they do. These remarkable offspring are examples of the miraculous adaptability of the natural world.

Narluga

In the 1980s, an Inuit hunter from western Greenland killed an unusual-looking whale. It seemed to have the front fins of a beluga and the tail of a narwhal. And instead of being white like a beluga or mottled like a narwhal, its skin was grey. The hunter had never seen anything quite like it. He was so intrigued that he kept the skull. When experts examined it, they realised the skull belonged to a rare kind of creature – a narluga – with a narwhal mother and a beluga father.

Although narwhal-beluga crosses are rare, they are not unheard of. In fact, the Indigenous people of western Greenland have a word for them: *itorsaq*.

In 2018, a young male narwhal was seen travelling with a group of beluga whales in the St Lawrence River. It's thought he had been adopted into the pod.

OUR CHANGING WORLD

In recent years, many animals have been forced to alter their habits as a result of climate change and the destruction of habitats. Species that wouldn't normally interact have been thrown together, meaning that crossbreeding is becoming more common. It's possible that some hybrid animals might be able to adapt more easily to our changing world than their parents.

Pizzly Bear

As our planet warms up, grizzly bears from Alaska and Canada are moving northwards, bringing them into contact with polar bears. In some cases, the two species mate, producing pizzly bears with a mix of features from both parents.

Mystery Monkey

In Borneo in 2017, a monkey was discovered that appeared to be a cross between two species – the silvery langur and the proboscis monkey – that have been forced together as forest habitats shrink. Most hybrid animals can't have babies, but this monkey was spotted nursing a youngster.

At the moment, nobody knows for sure if narlugas can reproduce and have babies of their own.

Tanabeak

In 2020, a bird-watcher in Pennsylvania, USA, came across a rare bird no-one had seen before: it looked like a rose-breasted grosbeak, but it sang like a scarlet tanager. It turned out to be a cross between the two different species.

Living Lights

Some special kinds of creature can glow in the dark. This 'living light', or bioluminescence, is unusual among land animals, but surprisingly three-quarters of sea creatures produce their own light. However, some ocean light shows are much rarer than others . . .

Sea of Stars

On certain beaches in the tropics, as the waves lap against the shore at night, millions of glittering specks of light can appear, like twinkling galaxies. The shimmering lights are caused by shoals of luminous plankton, known to gather in warm-water lagoons. These glowing bays are rare, fragile habitats: there are only a handful of them in the world, most located in the Caribbean and the Indian Ocean.

Bioluminescent beaches, where glowing plankton gather, are found in warm-water bays with narrow openings to the sea.

The most common plankton that light up the ocean are called dinoflagellates. Each no bigger than a pencil point, they produce light using chemicals inside their tiny bodies.

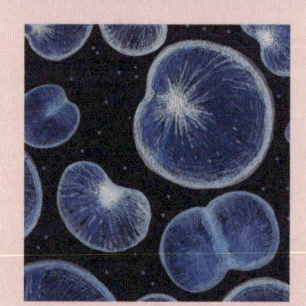

Party Trick

For the ancient Romans, a dinner-party delicacy was a shellfish called the piddock clam, which squirted a luminous slime. To the delight of guests, the lips of anyone who ate one turned a glowing green! Today, this clam is endangered in parts of Europe.

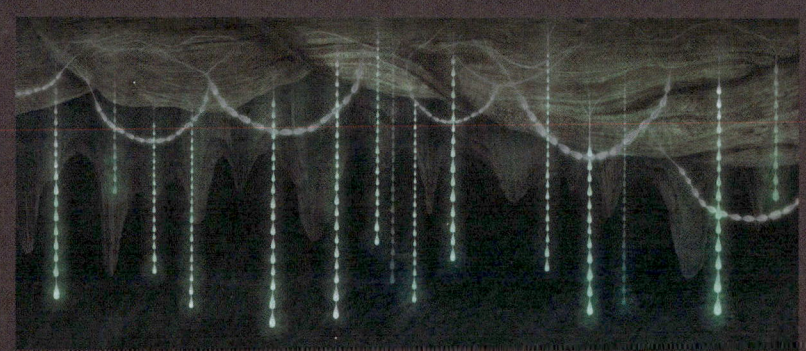

Light Show

The Waitomo Caves in New Zealand are home to some rare and spectacular glow-worms that light up the dark caverns like a roof of stars. These glowing creatures are not actually worms, but maggots: the baby larvae of a type of fly. The hungry youngsters glow to lure other insects, which they eat.

It's difficult to predict when blooms of glowing plankton will appear, so a sight like this is a special, perhaps once-in-a-lifetime, experience.

The lights of the plankton switch on when they are disturbed, like security lights. This glow attracts predators towards any creatures that feed on the plankton.

Flashing Fireflies

In the Great Smoky Mountains of the USA lives a rare type of creature, the synchronous firefly, which has a unique pattern of flashes. Unlike most other fireflies, the males of this species flash in unison with each other, probably so the females can be sure they're replying to their own kind.

Glowing Squid

Firefly squid normally live in the deep ocean, making them difficult to see. However, at certain times of year, in Japan's Toyama Bay, they are forced to the surface by the current and the shape of the sea floor.

Exploding Toads

In 2005, a pond on the outskirts of Hamburg, Germany, became the centre of a gruesome mystery. The toads that lived here began to swell up and explode for no apparent reason. Scientists were puzzled, and the strange case attracted attention from across the world . . .

A Murder of Crows

The remains of about a thousand toads were discovered near the 'Pool of Death'. They had swollen up to three times their normal size, then burst open. What could be causing these strange events? Perhaps a poison in the water, or a quick-spreading virus? But when scientists tested pond samples, they found nothing unusual. It was only when an expert examined the toads that he hit upon an answer. He found beak marks on their backs and realised their livers were missing. It seemed likely some clever crows had learned how to peck out the toads' nutritious livers while avoiding their toxic skin. When toads are attacked, they puff themselves up in self-defence. However, because of their injuries, this swelling caused them to explode!

Strange cases of exploding toads have been reported in other countries too, including in Denmark, Belgium and the USA.

Exploding Ants

It's not just toads that occasionally explode. If their nest is threatened by invading insects, some Malaysian exploding worker ants blow themselves up, sacrificing their lives to protect the colony. They contract the muscles of their abdomen, bursting a pair of poison-filled glands. These fire out a poisonous, sticky goo that snares the intruders.

Whale of a Bang

When a whale dies and begins to decompose, gases can build up in its stomach, causing an explosion if the pressure becomes too great. In 2004, a dead sperm whale was being carried on the back of a trailer to a research centre. Halfway through its journey the body exploded, showering cars and passers-by with stinking whale innards.

Curious Colours

Everyone knows that penguins are black and white, and that tigers are orange with black stripes . . . But the natural world never ceases to surprise us, and every so often, a creature is born that stands out in the most unique way.

Black Penguin

There are many different types of penguin, but they all have dark backs and white bellies. This 'countershading' may help them stay hidden from predators while diving for fish. They blend in with the dark water when seen from above, and with the bright sky when glimpsed from below. This patterning is found in all penguin species . . . so it was a huge surprise when, in 2019, wildlife photographers spotted an emperor penguin that was almost completely black. This extraordinary bird might be the only one of its kind. It probably has a special condition called melanism, which means it has high amounts of melanin – a natural pigment that gives colour to feathers, fur or skin.

Blue Lobster

Once in a blue moon, a blue lobster comes along! Most American lobsters are a murky brown colour, going red when cooked, but one in every two million is a vibrant blue. This rare condition is caused by an excess of a particular type of protein.

White Tiger

One in ten thousand wild tigers is white instead of orange, because it doesn't have colour pigments in its fur.

White Giraffe

Similar to a white tiger, a white giraffe doesn't have the skin pigments that give other giraffes their colours. In Kenya in 2020, the world's only known white giraffe was fitted with a GPS tracker so that rangers can keep a protective eye on him.

In 2010, a photographer visiting the island of South Georgia snapped an all-black king penguin that amazed experts.

Among a crowd of black-and-white penguins, the all-black emperor was discovered in Atka Bay, Antarctica, in 2019.

Black Chicken

The Ayam cemani is a rare breed of chicken from Indonesia. It has a certain gene that causes not only its feathers, but also its comb, beak, feet and even flesh and bones to be black! These unusual birds have been kept as pets for centuries.

Yellow Cardinal

Common in North America, the northern cardinal is famous for its bright red feathers. But very occasionally, a mustard-yellow cardinal crops up. Only about one in a million has this special colouring.

Pink Grasshopper

Grasshoppers are usually green or brown so they can blend in with their habitats. But sometimes, a rare gene causes a startling pink colour. In 2023 in Wales, a man was pruning flowers when he spotted a pink grasshopper at the bottom of his garden.

Amazing Migrations

Many animals make astonishing journeys in search of food, mates or warmer weather. Some manage to cover thousands of miles, often through harsh environments. Catching a glimpse of these remarkable creatures as they travel is a rare and special sight.

Wandering gliders follow the seasonal rains, travelling in search of shallow pools in which to lay their eggs.

These intrepid travellers migrate in huge swarms, sometimes numbering several thousand . . . but you have to be in the right place at the right time to see them.

A Dazzle of Dragonflies

The wandering glider, also called the globe skimmer, is one of the most impressive insects on the planet. This species is not uncommon – in fact, it's the most widespread dragonfly in the world – but it is known for performing a feat that is incredibly rare in the animal kingdom. This mini marvel, with its wingspan of only eight centimetres, makes a mammoth migration, further than any other insect. Some families of wandering gliders make round trips of up to 18,000 kilometres every year, from India to Africa and back again.

Monarch Butterflies

Each autumn in North America, clouds of flame-winged butterflies begin an epic journey south to Mexico and California in search of somewhere warm to spend the winter. Once, they flocked in their millions, but lately their numbers have fallen due to shrinking habitats, harmful pesticides and climate change. These iconic butterflies are becoming more and more rare, but efforts are being made to save them.

Christmas Island Crabs

One of the most incredible natural spectacles takes place each year on Christmas Island, in the Pacific. At the beginning of the rainy season, tens of millions of red crabs leave their forest homes and head for the coast to find a mate. These marching hordes of brightly coloured crustaceans carpet the streets and stop traffic. It is the largest land migration of any creature on Earth.

Some of the dragonflies mate and have babies along the way – it takes four generations to complete the round trip.

Some individuals hitch a lift on the winds, flying up to 6,000 kilometres on their leg of the journey across the open waters of the Indian Ocean.

Massive Murmurations

A murmuration is a wonder of nature: a huge flock of birds that fly together in whirling, swooping, ever-changing patterns in the air. The flock seems to move as one, in unison, as a rippling mass that looks like billowing smoke.

In the Northern Territory of Australia, these beautiful birds sometimes gather in groups of up to 100,000.

Flocking in large numbers protects the budgies from birds of prey: it is hard for a hawk to focus on a particular target among a swirling mass of feathers.

Jewels of the Outback

In the Australian Outback, flocks of emerald-green budgerigars swoop above the hot, dry landscapes. These parrots are always on the move, following the rains, feeding on grass seed and drinking at waterholes. Every ten years or so, a particularly wet season might cause budgie numbers to boom, causing flocks of a staggering size. As the warm sun rises over a waterhole, the birds begin to arrive – at first in small groups, then in their thousands as a twittering tornado. They duck and dive in a vast swarm, making twisting, turning shapes in the clear-blue sky.

Budgies have been known to travel up to 500 kilometres in a single day in search of food and water.

Shower of Starlings

Starlings are famous for their huge, graceful murmurations. Their lightning-fast reactions allow them to turn in unison with their neighbours, never colliding. It is hard to predict when and where these astonishing aerial displays will occur, but since the 1920s Rome has been a starling hotspot. Each winter, millions of the birds flock to the city, dancing above the rooftops.

Feathered Horde

In Sub-Saharan Africa, farmers dread the appearance of a flock of red-billed queleas. These small, sparrow-like songbirds gather in their millions in spectacular clouds so vast they can take five hours to pass overhead. As they move across the savannahs, they devour grass seed and crops.

Blotting Out the Sun

Not so long ago in North America, passenger pigeons roamed in awe-inspiring crowds that darkened the skies. One flock was so big it was said to have taken 14 hours to pass by. It was estimated to measure nearly 500 kilometres long (the width of Great Britain) and contain 3.5 billion pigeons! Sadly, these record-breaking birds were hunted to extinction in the early 1900s.

Unique Wild Places

From the boiling river of Peru to the deepest cave on Earth, from volcanic lakes of acid to impenetrable forests of stone, a few locations on the globe are so unusual that they challenge our understanding of the natural world. These rare wonders – remarkable rivers, strange lakes, amazing caves and weird volcanoes – showcase our planet at its most breathtaking.

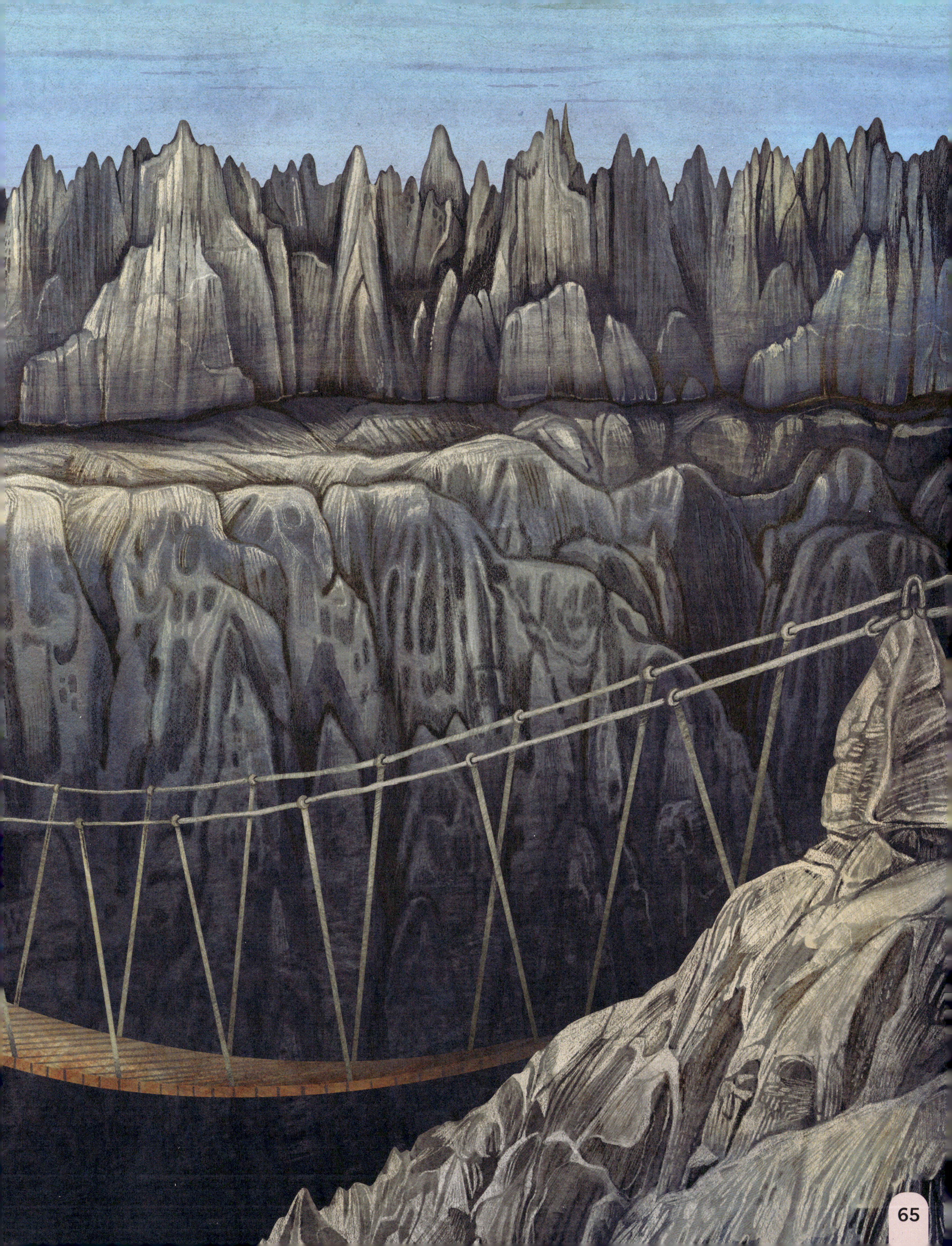

Remarkable Rivers

There are hundreds of thousands of rivers in the world – they flow through nearly every country, carrying fresh water from the mountains to the sea. Many of these waterways are remarkable for their size, their power or their natural beauty, but some are particularly unusual.

Rainbow River

In central Colombia there is a river famous for its rainbow colours. Running through an area of striking beauty, where the Amazon rainforest meets the Andes mountains, the Caño Cristales is a fast-flowing stream dotted with pools and waterfalls. For a few weeks each year, between September and November, the river becomes a liquid rainbow, turning shades of red, orange, blue, yellow and green. This explosion of colour is due to a mossy plant that grows on the riverbed. For most of the year the plant is green, but at the end of the rainy season it turns a bright red.

Boiling River

Deep in the Peruvian rainforest is an extraordinary river like no other. Known as Shanay-Timpishka, or the Boiling River, this 6-kilometre stretch of water is warmed by underground hot springs until it bubbles and steams. The water can reach temperatures of over 90° Celsius – hot enough to boil an egg, or kill any creature that falls into it!

The colours of the Rainbow River are at their best when the sun is shining and the water level is just right.

The plant that gives the water its colour is very rare – it grows only in this region, thanks to the mineral-rich rocks.

Underground River

Beneath Mexico's Yucatán Peninsula is an enormous network of caves and tunnels, carved out of the rock by trickling rainwater long ago. The Sac Actun river, which twists and turns for 153 kilometres through these shadowy caverns, is the longest underground river in the world. Divers and snorkellers explore the crystal-clear waters, bathed in light that filters down from holes in the limestone ceiling.

Strange Lakes

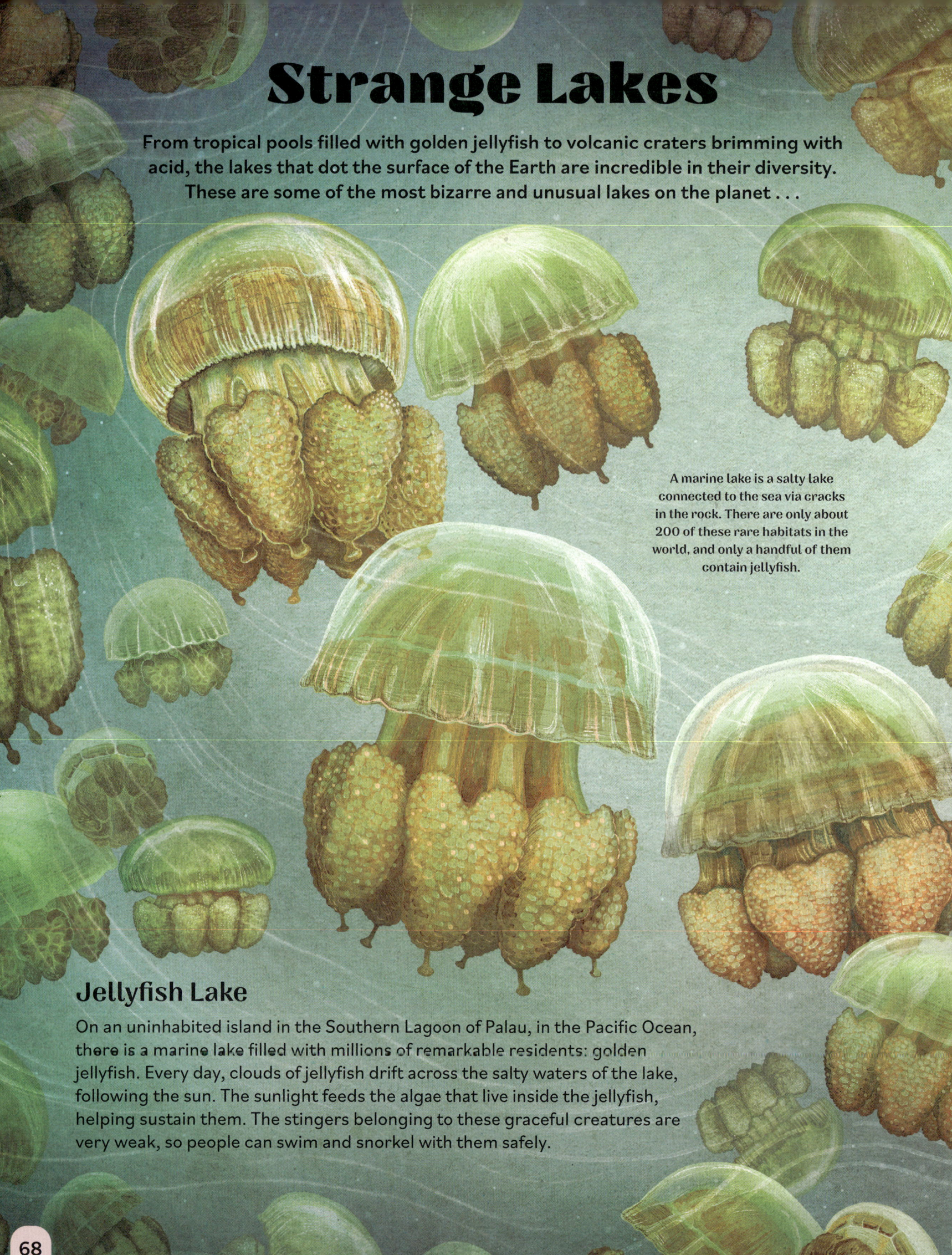

From tropical pools filled with golden jellyfish to volcanic craters brimming with acid, the lakes that dot the surface of the Earth are incredible in their diversity. These are some of the most bizarre and unusual lakes on the planet . . .

A marine lake is a salty lake connected to the sea via cracks in the rock. There are only about 200 of these rare habitats in the world, and only a handful of them contain jellyfish.

Jellyfish Lake

On an uninhabited island in the Southern Lagoon of Palau, in the Pacific Ocean, there is a marine lake filled with millions of remarkable residents: golden jellyfish. Every day, clouds of jellyfish drift across the salty waters of the lake, following the sun. The sunlight feeds the algae that live inside the jellyfish, helping sustain them. The stingers belonging to these graceful creatures are very weak, so people can swim and snorkel with them safely.

Palau's Jellyfish Lake has several layers of water that don't mix. Fifteen metres beneath the surface is a deadly layer where the pitch-black water is filled with toxic substances that could poison divers!

Bubblegum Pool

Lake Hillier, which lies on a small island off the coast of Western Australia, looks like a pool of liquid bubblegum. Its peculiar pink colour is caused by the unusual algae and bacteria that live in its extremely salty water.

Lake of Lava

Mount Nyiragongo, in the Democratic Republic of the Congo, is one of the most active volcanoes in the world. At its peak is a 2-kilometre-wide crater that contains the biggest lava lake on the planet.

Acid Lagoon

At the top of Indonesia's Ijen volcano, on the island of Java, is a lake whose turquoise waters look inviting . . . but you wouldn't want to swim here. This is the world's largest acid lake, containing a powerful brew stronger than battery acid – so harmful it could easily dissolve human flesh or melt through a steel barrel.

Ocean Oddities

The ocean covers nearly three-quarters of the Earth's surface and is home to many natural wonders. Much of this vast watery world is unexplored by humans, so we are still discovering its secrets – from the bizarre pools of brine that lie deep beneath the waves to the strange foamy swells that sometimes occur along coastlines.

The whipped-up waves in Yamba were not dangerous, so locals poured onto the beach to join the foam party.

Foamy Seas

One day in August 2007, people living in Yamba, in Australia's New South Wales, woke to find their beaches blanketed in huge amounts of foam, whipped up overnight by storms off the coast. This unusual foamy swell was caused not by a giant spillage of bubble bath, but by plankton. When these tiny sea creatures die, they release proteins into the water which, when stirred up by strong waves and winds, make foam. In Yamba, the combination of large blooms of plankton with powerful waves led to a tsunami of frothy bubbles, giving the region the nickname the 'Cappuccino Coast'.

Sometimes, fertilisers, industrial waste and sewage are washed into the ocean, triggering blooms of foam-producing plankton. However, foamy seas are not always caused by pollution.

Although sea foam is not uncommon, such a huge quantity is a rare phenomenon.

Brine Pool

These rare, mysterious, eerily calm underwater lakes are found on the sea floor, hundreds of metres below the surface. A brine pool is filled with dense water up to eight times saltier than the surrounding ocean. Giant mussels and shrimps gather around the edge, but few creatures enter the toxic brine itself. Those that do usually die a painful death, starved of oxygen.

Brinicle

These peculiar icy columns are found only in extremely cold seas, such as the ocean around Antarctica. As ice forms on the surface, it leaves behind dense, very salty water, which sinks quickly, creating a frozen finger. When it touches the seabed, the ice spreads out, killing any creatures caught in its wintry grasp.

Whirlpool

In some oceans, where two currents meet, they can form a swirling vortex known as a maelstrom, or whirlpool. This can be dangerous, pulling small boats into its spiralling funnel. One of the world's biggest whirlpools – the Old Sow – sometimes appears off the coast of New Brunswick, Canada, and can measure up to about 75 metres across.

Amazing Caves

Some natural wonders lie deep underground. Carved out by water millions of years ago, these awe-inspiring, record-breaking caves offer a rare glimpse into a strange, subterranean world.

Deepest Cave

The limestone hills of Abkhazia, to the northwest of Georgia, are home to four of the deepest caves in the world, including the record-busting Veryovkina Cave. From its narrow entrance in a hillside, a series of craggy tunnels descend deeper and deeper towards the centre of the Earth. Exploring this underground labyrinth is a difficult, dangerous business. The cave was first discovered in 1968, but it wasn't until 2018 that a team of cave explorers (speleologists) made it down to a record depth of 2,212 metres.

Exploring the cave is similar to climbing Mount Everest in reverse. It takes at least three days to descend and the same again to return to the surface!

Descending into this pitch-black maze is very risky. Rockfalls and flash floods are just some of the many hazards faced in these underground tunnels.

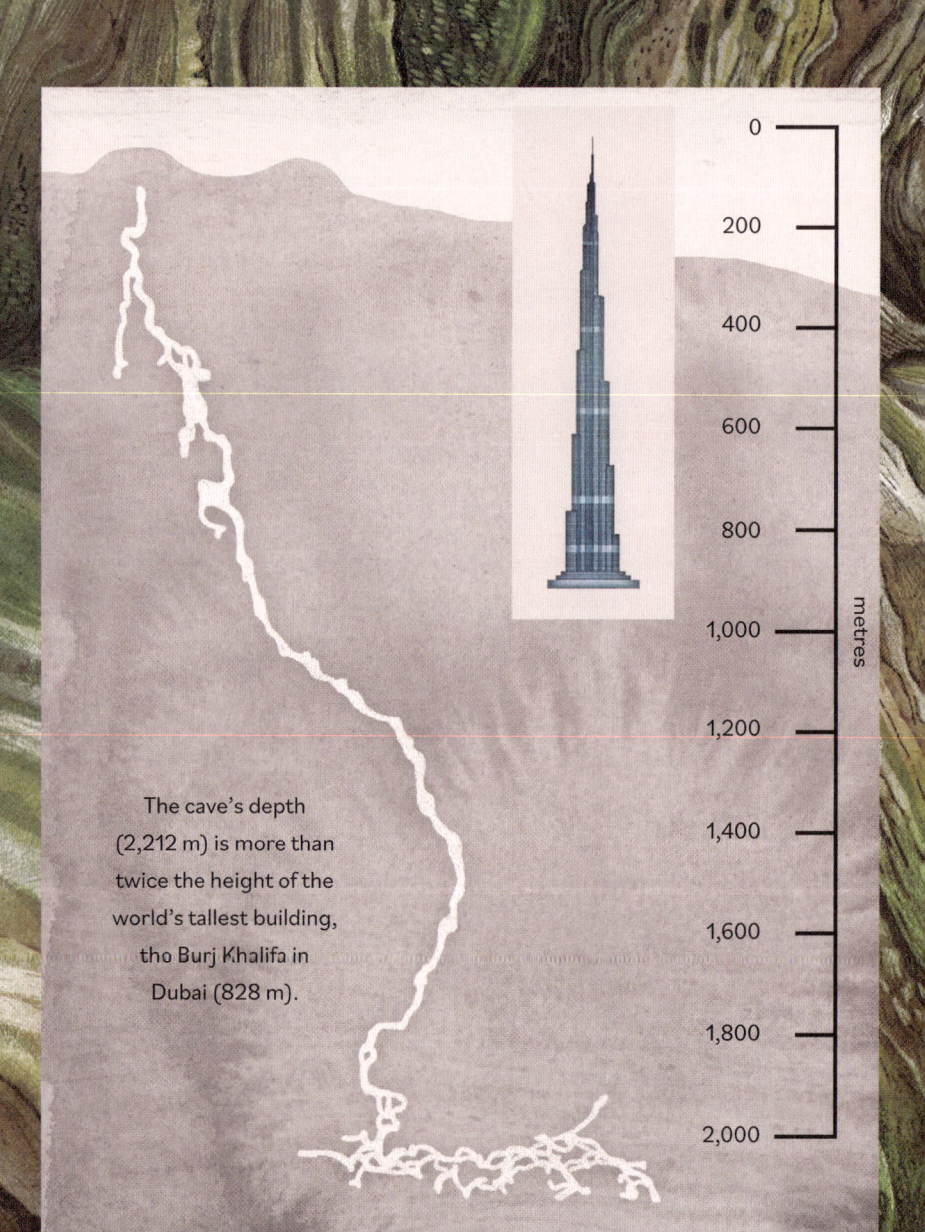

The cave's depth (2,212 m) is more than twice the height of the world's tallest building, the Burj Khalifa in Dubai (828 m).

The tunnels descend almost vertically through the limestone rock, opening out into a complex maze towards the bottom.

Largest Cave

Beneath the lush forests of central Vietnam lie the cavernous halls of Hang Son Doong. This is the biggest cave on Earth, with a volume of 38.5 million cubic metres – close to 18 times the volume of London's O2 arena! As well as containing its own underground river and a rainforest, Hang Son Doong is home to some of the tallest stalagmites in the world, measuring 80 metres.

Biggest Single Chamber

In southern China's Gebihe cave system is a chamber so vast you could fly a Boeing 747 jet through it. The Miao Room cavern can be reached only via an underground stream. It measures 852 metres long by 191 metres wide, with a ceiling height of nearly 300 metres in places – as tall as the Eiffel Tower.

Longest Cave System

The Mammoth Cave network in Kentucky, USA, is a maze of limestone tunnels and chambers, some dripping with stalactites. This is the longest cave system in the world: so far, more than 686 kilometres of passageways have been explored, with new tunnels still being discovered.

Rare Rocks

In certain places around the world, nature has produced some incredible rock formations. Sculpted by the wind and rain, or by fiery forces deep within the Earth, these unique wonders tell the story of our planet's past.

Fingal's Cave

On the southern shore of Scotland's Isle of Staffa is a landmark that looks like something from a fantasy world. The towering walls of this sea cave are lined with huge hexagonal columns, formed 60 million years ago when a vast sheet of lava cracked as it cooled. The same lava flow also created the famous Giant's Causeway, which lies across the water in Northern Ireland. Legend has it that the two sites marked either end of a colossal ancient walkway, built by giants!

Devil's Tower

Jutting 264 metres above the landscape, the Devil's Tower – or Bear Lodge – in Wyoming, USA, is an astonishing natural feature, formed about 50 million years ago from a plug of magma. This majestic landmark is sacred to many Indigenous groups, including the Lakota and Cheyenne peoples. Traditional stories say it sprang up to lift some children out of reach of a giant bear, who scratched grooves in the sides with its claws.

Eye of the Sahara

From the ground it could easily be missed, but from above this strange circular pattern looks like an enormous bullseye. This 45-kilometre-wide rock formation in the Sahara Desert looks like the landing site of a flying saucer. In fact, the rings are the remains of a rocky dome worn away over millions of years. This unique structure has fascinated scientists since it was first photographed by astronauts in the 1960s.

The cavernous interior echoes and emphasises the sound of crashing waves, inspiring artists and composers.

The cave extends for 82 metres and its arched ceiling reaches 22 metres above sea level.

Kjeragbolten

If you're scared of heights, this place is not for you. The Kjeragbolten in Norway is a huge boulder wedged between two cliffs, a dizzying kilometre above sea level. It's thought to have been left there by a glacier during the last ice age. Despite its forbidding appearance, it is possible to walk (or crawl) onto the rock without special equipment, though it's a challenging hike to get there.

Tsingy National Park

In west Madagascar, a forest of stone rises from the earth, its needle-sharp spires reaching skywards. These strange spikes were shaped millions of years ago as water wore away parts of a limestone slab. The name 'Tsingy' means 'where one cannot walk barefoot' - appropriate considering the treacherous terrain! Home to many types of lemur, this otherworldly place is the largest stone forest on the planet, covering 600 square kilometres.

Weird Volcanoes

When you imagine a volcano, you probably think of red-hot lava spewing from a mountaintop. But not all volcanoes are alike: some are uniquely strange, others are jaw-dropping in their fiery potential.

These glowing blue streams are not actually lava, but sulphuric fire.

Supervolcano

Beneath North America's Yellowstone National Park lurks a sleeping giant: a monster volcano so powerful that, last time it erupted, it sent a pillar of scorching ash and molten rock thousands of metres into the air, plunging the continent into darkness. This previous eruption was 640,000 years ago. Thankfully, the Yellowstone volcano is monitored very closely, and scientists don't believe we are due another big eruption any time soon.

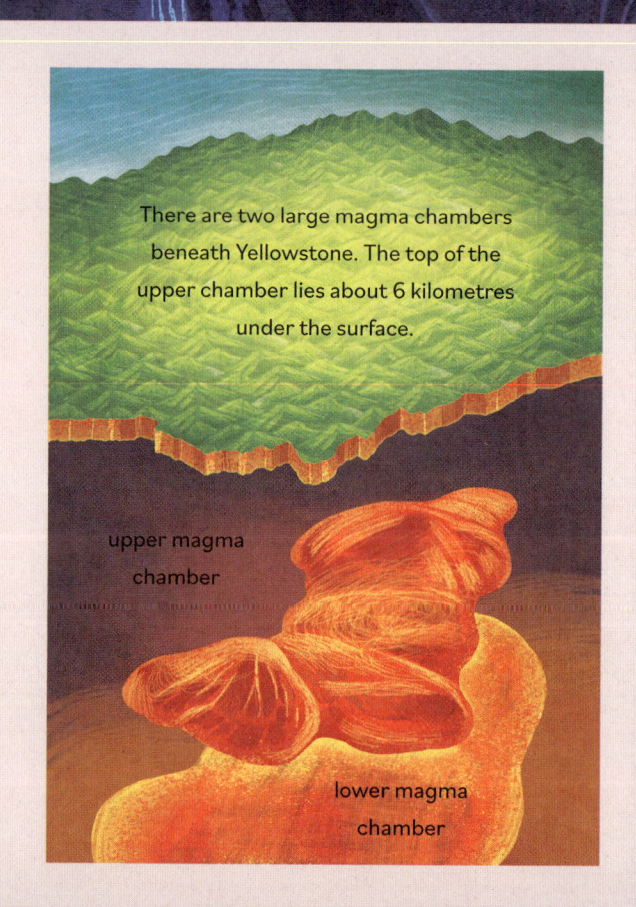

There are two large magma chambers beneath Yellowstone. The top of the upper chamber lies about 6 kilometres under the surface.

upper magma chamber

lower magma chamber

Blue Fire

Indonesia's Ijen volcano, on the island of Java, is remarkable not only for its lake of acid (see page 69), but also for the electric-blue flames that burst from vents near its crater. This strange fire is caused by a gas called sulphur, which burns blue when it meets the air. This gas is forced out of the volcano at high pressure, at scorching temperatures of up to 600° Celsius. After firing into the air in a burst of blue flame, the sulphur transforms into a burning liquid, flowing downhill as a river of sapphire light.

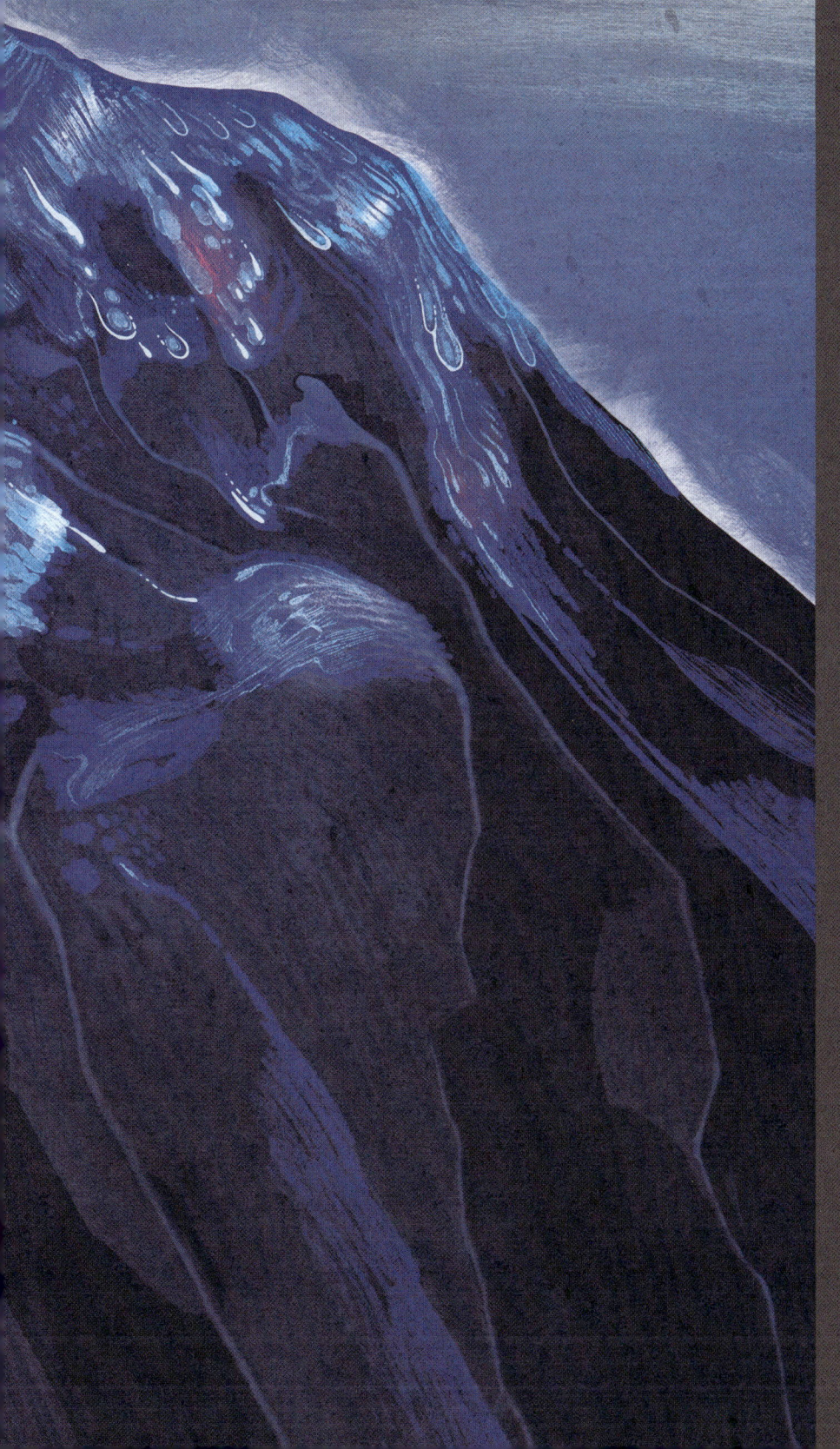

FIRE AND ICE

If you think of the frozen continent of Antarctica, a fiery volcano might not be the first thing that springs to mind. But Antarctica is actually home to more than a hundred volcanoes. Most of them are extinct, but Mount Erebus is the southernmost active volcano on the planet, and one of the very few to have a lava lake in its crater. (Out of more than 1,500 active volcanoes worldwide, only about eight have lava lakes).

Towering above the frozen landscape, Erebus breathes and bubbles, sending steam and chunks of molten rock into the air.

On the snowy slopes, a network of strange and intricate ice caves have formed, melted by hot gases escaping from volcanic vents.

Glossary

Algae Tiny, plant-like living things

Asteroid A small rocky object that orbits the Sun

Astronomer A scientist who studies stars, planets and the night sky

Astronomical Relating to space

Atmosphere Layers of gases that surround the Earth

Aurora Colourful displays of light that appear in the night sky, usually above the poles

Bioluminescence The ability of certain plants and animals to produce their own light

Botanist Someone who studies plants

Canopy The leafy roof of a forest or tree

Carnivorous Plant A plant that traps and consumes insects and small animals

Carrion Beetle A beetle that feeds and lays its eggs on dead animals

Core (of a star) The hot, dense centre of a star

Crossbreeding When two different species mate and produce young

Element A pure substance made of only one kind of atom

Elusive Rare, or hard to find

Fungi Living things such as mushrooms and mould, which grow in warm, damp places, and are neither plants nor animals

Galaxy A huge gathering of stars and planets

Gas A substance that can be invisible, which spreads out to fill a space (air is a mixture of different gases)

Gene Found inside the cells of living things, genes are like instruction manuals that determine how things grow and develop

Habitat The place where an animal or plant usually lives

Hybrid Animal A creature whose parents are from different species

Indigenous Directly descended from the earliest inhabitants of a particular place

Lagoon A shallow body of water that is blocked off from the sea by a natural barrier such as a reef

Magma Molten rock from beneath Earth's surface

Magnetic Field (Earth's) An invisible shield that protects our planet from harmful radiation

Mesopotamia The region of ancient West Asia between the Tigris and Euphrates rivers

Meteorite A chunk of rock from space that lands on Earth's surface

Microwave Radiation A type of invisible energy that travels through the air in waves

Migration (Animals) When animals move from one place another at certain times of year, to find food, mates, or relief from extreme weather

Mirage An image of something that isn't really there, sometimes caused by light rays being bent or reflected

Molecule A tiny particle made up of two or more atoms joined together

Naturalist A person who studies the natural world

Nectar A sweet liquid produced by flowers

Nutrients The things in food that help plants and animals grow

Omen A sign or warning of a future event

Orbit The path of an object in space around another

Particle Something extremely tiny, too small to see with the naked eye

Pesticide A type of chemical designed to kill or repel insects

Phenomenon An unusual or interesting event

Plankton Tiny plants and animals that float in the oceans

Plasma A super-hot, highly charged, glowing type of gas

Pollinate The process of moving pollen between flowers, or within a flower, to help plants make seeds and reproduce

Portent (See 'Omen')

Prop Root A root that grows down from above the ground, helping to anchor a plant to the earth

Putrid Rotten and foul-smelling

Sacred Regarded with great respect by a particular religion or group

Savannah A large grassland with scattered trees and shrubs

Solar Wind A stream of highly charged particles that flow from the Sun

Species A group of living things that share common characteristics and are able to interbreed

Subterranean Underground

Tropics The warm regions of Earth that lie either side of the Equator

Wars of the Roses A series of battles in England in the 1400s fought between the families of York and Lancaster for control of the throne

Index

A
Abkhazia 72
Africa 60, 63
air 17, 24, 26, 27, 29, 30, 31, 38, 41, 62, 76, 77
Alaska 23, 53
algae 33, 68, 69
ancestors 6
ancient China 12, 14
ancient Greece 14, 46
ancient Romans 54
animals 7, 34, 36, 37, 40, 42, 47, 48, 50, 51, 52, 53, 54, 55, 56, 57, 58, 59, 60, 61, 62, 63
Antarctica 59, 71, 77
Aristotle 46
asteroids 17
astronauts 74
astronomers 14, 18
atmosphere 10, 17, 20, 22, 23, 24, 26, 27
Attenborough, Sir David 42
auroras 22, 23
    Aurora Australis
      (Southern Lights) 22
    Aurora Borealis
      (Northern Lights) 22
Australia 29, 31, 47, 51, 62, 69, 70

B
bacteria 69
ball lightning 6, 28, 29
Belgium 57
bioluminescence 7, 34, 46, 47, 54
black hole 19
Bolivia 37
Borneo 34, 43, 53
botanist 47

C
Canada 53, 71
caves 54, 64, 67, 72, 73, 74, 75, 77
China 73
Christmas Island 61
climate change 40, 53, 61
cloud formations 30, 31
clouds 20, 24, 28, 30, 31
Colombia 66
comets 9, 14, 15, 17
corona 13
countershading 58
crossbreeding 52, 53
Cuba 23

D
Democratic Republic of the Congo 69
Denmark 57
deserts 36, 74
Dubai 72

E
Earth 10, 11, 12, 13, 14, 15, 17, 22, 38, 44, 61, 64, 70, 72, 73
eclipses 6, 9, 12, 13
  partial 13
  solar 12, 13
  total 6, 12, 13
Ecuador 41
electricity 23, 26, 28
elements 19
England 23, 29
Europe 16

F
Finland 23, 32
flowers 7, 34, 36, 37, 44, 45
forest fires 10
forests 7, 16, 47, 53, 61, 73
France 50
Franklin, Benjamin 26
fungi 34, 46, 47

G
galaxies 18
gases 15, 18, 22, 26, 29, 57, 77
Genghis Khan 14
genes 59
Germany 48, 56
Giotto spacecraft 15
gravity 18, 19
Great Britain 31, 63
Greenland 52

H
habitat destruction 53
Halley, Edmond 14
hybrid animals 53

I
Inca people 12
India 34, 37, 38, 60
Indigenous groups 74
Indonesia 7, 44, 47, 59, 69, 77

J
Japan 30, 47, 51, 55

K
Kenya 48-58

L
lagoons 54
lakes 27, 32, 51, 64, 68, 69, 71, 77
    underwater 71
lava 69, 74, 76, 77

M
Madagascar 75
magma 74, 76
magnetic field (Earth's) 22
mating 60
melanism 58
Mesopotamia 12
meteor air burst 17
meteorite 16
Mexico 37, 38, 61, 67
microwave radiation 29
migrations 37, 60, 61
Milky Way 18
mirage 27
molecules 22, 26
Moon 10, 11, 13
  'blue moon' 10
  moonbow 25
  moon dogs 24
  penumbra 13
  phases 10, 11
  'super blue moon' 11
  supermoon 11
  umbra 13
mountains 23, 30, 33, 37, 39, 42, 55, 66
murmurations 62, 63

N
naturalists 42
nectar 37, 42
New Zealand 54
North America 59, 61, 63
Northern Ireland 74
Norway 23, 75
nutrients 38, 42

O
oceans 27, 31, 34, 40, 51, 54, 55, 60, 68, 70, 71
orbit 11, 13, 15

P
Palau 69
Peru 7, 37, 41, 64, 66
phenomena 20, 26, 27, 29, 50, 71
Philippines 42
planets 15, 19
plankton 54, 55, 70, 71
plants 7, 34, 36, 37, 40, 42, 43, 44, 45, 47, 66
  carnivorous 7, 42
plasma 26, 29
poles 22, 23
pollination 36, 44, 47
pollution 71
predators 55, 58
pressure 18, 57
prey 43
prop roots 39

R
rainforests 44, 66, 73
reproduction 52
resin 34, 40, 41
rivers 7, 16, 64, 66, 67
rock formations 74, 75
Russia 16, 17

S
St Elmo's Fire 26, 27
savannahs 63
scientists 16, 17, 23, 28, 29, 39, 46, 51, 56, 74, 76
Scotland 50, 74
sea foam 70, 71
Serbia 51
Siberia 16, 32
snow 32, 33
Socotra 34, 40
solar winds 20, 22, 23
South Africa 43
South America 12, 41
South Georgia 59
space 9, 16, 18, 19
speleologists 72
stalactites 73
stalagmites 73
star dust 19
stars 9, 18, 19
subterranean
Sun 12, 13, 15, 19, 22, 23, 24, 31
    sun dogs 24, 25
supernovas 18, 19

T
telescopes 15, 18
Transit of Venus 15
trees 7, 16, 17, 34, 38, 39, 40, 41, 46
tropics 54

U
UFOs 28, 30
UK 16
USA 32, 33, 37, 43, 48, 50, 51, 55, 57, 73, 74, 76

V
Venus 15
Vietnam 73
volcanic craters 68, 69, 77
volcanic eruption 10, 76
volcanoes 7, 64, 69, 76, 77

W
Wales 41, 59
water 24, 27, 30, 38, 45, 54, 56, 58, 62, 63, 66, 67, 69, 70, 71, 72, 74, 75
Wars of the Roses 25
weather 20, 27, 60
whirlpools 71